ZION
NATIONAL · PARK

Towers of Stone

By J. L. Crawford

Z I O N

Art Direction by
Sarah Fine

Design/Production by
Brookie Branch, Katrina Selzer,
and Joanne Station

Edited by
Angela Tripp and Carey Vendrame

Editorial Assistance by
Teresa Roupe and Gilda Parodi-Swords

Review by
Denny Davies, National Park Service

© 1988, 1991, 1994 by
Zion Natural History Association
Zion National Park
Springdale, Utah 84767
(801) 772-3265
Jamie Gentry, Publisher
Published 1988. All rights reserved
Third Edition 1994

Albion Publishing Group
Santa Barbara, CA
(805) 963-6004
Lorie Bacon, Publisher

Printed in Hong Kong by
Everbest Printing Company, Ltd.
through Asiaprint/Everbest U.S.A.
ISBN 0-915630-33-8
(previously ISBN 1-880352-00-1)

Cover: The Watchman.
Inside front cover: The Virgin River with the Watchman in the background.
Previous page: Middle Fork of Taylor Creek in Kolob's Finger Canyons.

PHOTOGRAPHY

J. Cecil Alter: 11 inset, 13 top. *Frank Balthis:* 5. *Cindy Beaudett (NPS):* 19 bottom. *Dan Belknap:* cover, inside front cover-page–1. *Lynn Chamberlain:* 35 top, 50 middle. *Ralph Clevenger:* 7, 22 inset middle, 24 left, 25 bottom right, 29 top left, 29 bottom. *Ed Cooper:* front flap, 25 top left, 34–35. *J.L. Crawford:* 6 top, 18, 19 top, 20–21. *Wm. L. Crawford:* 8 top. *Clint Crawley, Images West Photography:* 49 bottom, 50 top. *Joseph Dombrosky:* 12 top. *Christine Fancher:* 27 top. *Howard Firm (NPS):*

12 bottom. *Jeff Henry:* 50 bottom. *Frank Jensen:* 2–3, 29 middle right, 38–39, 39 bottom right, 40 bottom, 42 left, 44 bottom, back cover. *Dewitt Jones:* 22–23, 22 inset left, 23 bottom, 25 top right, 26 left, 47. *John Jones:* 6 bottom, 45 bottom. *Mark Kelleher:* inside back cover, back flap. *Paul Leib:* 36 bottom right. *Dennis Mecham:* 54–55. *Cara Moore:* 9, 24 right, 25 bottom left, 37 top, 46. *NPS:* 52 bottom, 53. *B. "Moose" Peterson/WRP:* 49 top. *Putnam & Valentine:* 8–9, 10 inset. *Bill Ratcliffe:* 16 top,

31 right, 32 top left, center and right, 39 bottom left. *Joseph Romeo:* 32–33. *Jon Mark Stewart:* 23 top. *John Telford:* 14 bottom left, 27 bottom, 35 bottom, 39 top, 43, 48–49, 51, 52 top. *Tom Till:* 36 bottom left, 42 right. *Union Pacific:* 10–11. *Glenn Van Nimwegan:* 14 top and bottom right, 17, 28, 29 middle left, 30 left and right, 31 left, 33 top, 36 top, 40 top, 44–45, 45 top. *Dave Wappler:* 30 middle, 37 bottom, 38, 41. *Robert Winslow/Tom Stack & Associates:* 26 right. *Art Wolfe, Inc.:* 22–23 inset.

Dear Readers:

This publication has been made available by the Zion Natural History Association, a nonprofit corporation working in cooperation with the National Park Service.

This is only one of the many functions we perform to increase the quality of your visit to National Park Service areas. The association also awards scholarships, funds interpretive projects and scientific research, produces free publications, aids in museum and library activities, and helps with many other National Park Service programs.

The Zion Natural History Association is directed by a voluntary Board of Directors and is supported by the sale of publications, maps, and other interpretive items that visitors can purchase at a natural history association sales area. The association could not continue to assist the National Park Service without your support.

I wish to thank you, the visitor. Through your purchases you are part of the winning team effort to support the National Park Service. Also a special thank you to the Zion Natural History Association Board of Directors for its dedication and guidance.

In this publication we have made available a reorder card for your convenience. This card also serves as a Zion Natural History Association membership application. If you join, you will enjoy the benefits of membership and stay more informed of our progress and development in the years to come.

Gratefully yours,

Jamie Gentry

Jamie Gentry
Executive Director
Zion Natural
History Association

Author J.L. Crawford was 10 years old when the first graded roads were cut through Zion Canyon. He sold farm produce and photographs to tourists and tagged along behind the park's first naturalist. Crawford's first book, *Zion Album, A Nostalgic History of Zion,* was published by the Zion Natural History Association in 1986.

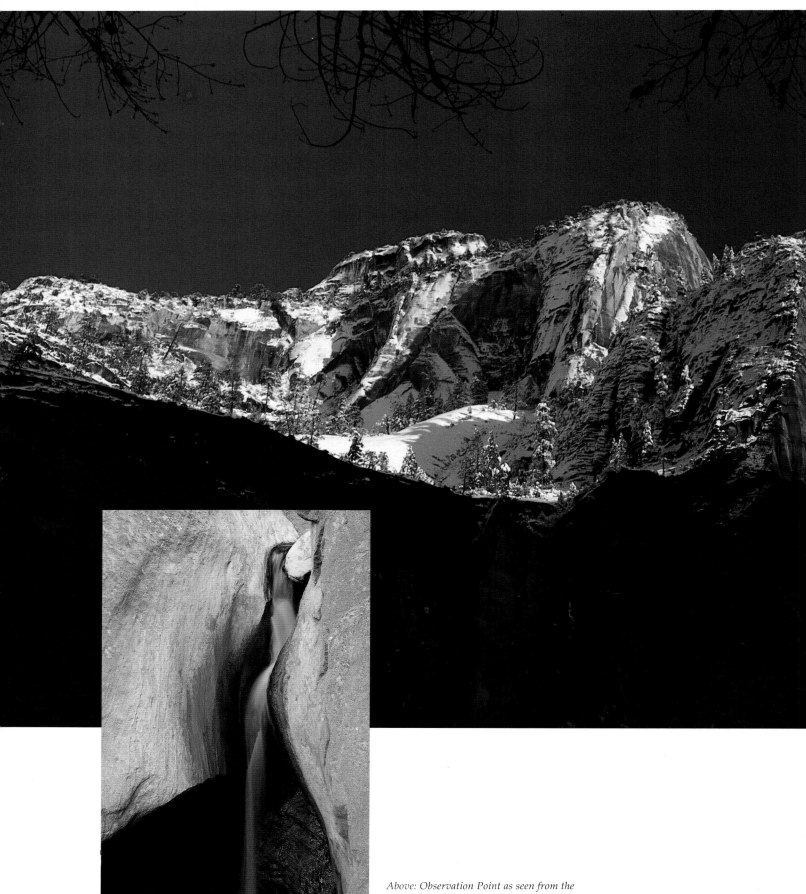

Above: Observation Point as seen from the Temple of Sinawava.
Left: One of Zion's many small tributaries.
Far right: Seed head of the yellow salsify, or goatsbeard, a very common and showy plant in Zion.

CONTENTS

*Right: The Zion Canyon road, early 1920s.
Below: Oak Creek Village, circa 1917. Today the area in the bottom left corner is the site of the Zion Canyon Visitor Center.*

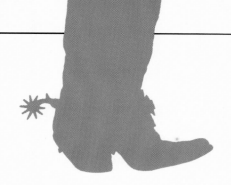

Chapter One

EARLY INHABITANTS

The first known residents of Zion were the Basket Makers. They were seminomadic Indians who eventually evolved into the Pueblo culture as their lifestyle became more sedentary and their means of subsistence changed from primarily hunting to growing and storing crops. The Pueblos, now known as Anasazi (Navajo for "Ancient Ones"), occupied Zion from A.D. 500 to about A.D. 1200. This culture began to decline earlier in the Zion area than it did in the center of the Anasazi region (an area called "Four Corners," where the borders of Utah, Arizona, New Mexico, and Colorado meet), probably due to pressure from enemies to the north and west. The elaborate pueblos common to the Four Corners area are not found here. Pictographs and petroglyphs have been found, along with a few food storage bins constructed of mud and stone. Archaeologists have unearthed the foundation of what appears to have been an extensive building that was constructed of mud and rocks—a multiroomed masonry pueblo that housed several families. Artifacts indicate that the occupants grew corn, squash, and beans and hunted turkey, deer, and bighorn sheep.

Following the Anasazi, several Paiute Indian subtribes occupied the region. They were of Shoshonean stock and were subject to the greater Ute tribe to the north, whose chief exacted annual tributes from the weaker tribes. Children were often taken as an offering when other commodities were lacking. This practice became more prevalent during the Spanish era, as the slave trade proved to be quite lucrative. Domination by the Utes, and frequent raids by Navajos from across the Colorado River had rendered the local Paiutes destitute by the time the Mormons took possession of the area.

A small subtribe called the Parrusits occupied the stretch of the Virgin River (they called it Pah-roos) below Zion Canyon. They had no permanent dwellings, but moved up and down the river and into adjacent areas seasonally, using their vast knowledge of wild food sources. The Parrusits did some farming along the river, but their diet consisted mostly of wild seeds, roots, insects, lizards, small mammals, and a wide range of

other wild foods.

The arrival of Mormon settlers displaced most Paiutes from the places they had long lived and gathered food. Some groups lost their identity entirely. Those Paiutes who remained adopted some of the ways of the new settlers. Today their descendants live in the area on reservations and in towns.

The first recorded visit to southwestern Utah by Europeans was made in 1776 by the Dominguez-Escalante expedition on its return from abandoning a quest to find a northern route to California. On the verge of starvation, the party followed the Hurricane Fault scarp southward and passed within 20 miles of Zion Canyon. The men noted the high mesas to the east but did no exploring.

Fifty years later, Jedediah Smith, with a party of 16 men, passed by in the tracks of the Spaniards. They were fur traders in search of beaver pelts but were more intent on finding a route to California, so they failed to find the canyon.

Several military and geographic explorations were carried out in the surrounding area before the arrival of the Mormons, but Zion remained largely unknown to them until 1858 when Nephi Johnson, a young missionary to the Indians and an interpreter for immigrant parties passing through the area, explored the upper Virgin River on Brigham Young's orders. The Mormons sought out areas rich in natural resources to build self-sufficient communities and expand their economic, cultural, and ecclesiastical interests.

Several communities, including Springdale, were soon established along the river, at the mouth of Zion Canyon. In 1863 Isaac Behunin, one of the Springdale settlers, built a cabin near the present site of the Zion Lodge where he farmed for several years.

Zion became known through the work of artists, photographers, and writers in the late 1800s and early 1900s. But the publicity Zion received had little effect on travel to the area because the roads were little more than trails.

In 1908 a U.S. government deputy surveyor named Leo Snow was hired to survey the township that included Zion Canyon. He was so impressed

with the scenery that in his report the following year he recommended that the canyon be designated a national monument. On July 31, 1909, a month after the letter reached the office of the secretary of the interior, President Taft signed a proclamation creating Mukuntuweap National Monument. Ten years later the name was changed to Zion National Monument and in 1919 Congress renamed the area Zion National Park.

The designation of the canyon as a national monument opened the way for making the region accessible, but changes were slow in coming. While the approach road to the canyon was still primarily on the flood plain of the river, the residents of Springdale and Zion were exploring the possibility of a road through Pine Creek that would shorten the distance to ranches, to timber areas, and to markets where they sold their farm produce.

One of the principal advocates of such a route was John Winder, who owned a ranch on the East Rim of Zion. A second-generation pioneer, Winder was a colorful character in Zion's history. He was an orphan without formal education who was described by a contemporary as being "tough as boiled owl."

Background photo: Utah Parks Company buses at the Temple of Sinawava.
Inset left: William Wylie operated this tourist camp in Zion Canyon from 1917–1923.
Inset right: Second-generation pioneer John Winder in Echo Canyon.

Around the turn of the century, Winder and his neighbors built a trail up the east wall to his ranch over which livestock could be driven. The trail is still maintained by the National Park Service as the East Rim Trail. But Winder had a shorter route that he used when he was in a hurry to get to or from the ranch. It was not a trail, but rather a shortcut through the narrow gorge of Pine Creek that necessitated some cliff scaling. This is the route over which he guided the engineers who surveyed the Zion Tunnel, although the tunnel itself does not follow Winder's route. The completion of the tunnel in 1930 brought Winder's greatest dream to fruition.

In 1917 the Wylie Way Camp was established. The Zion Lodge, operated by the Utah Parks Company, a subsidiary of the Union Pacific Railroad, replaced the camp in 1925. Zion became a national park in 1919. This new status brought about other improvements, including the completion of the Zion–Mt. Carmel Highway in 1930. The highway shortened the distance to Bryce Canyon by 70 miles, and to the Grand Canyon by 20 miles. Best of all, it eliminated a hazardous stretch of mountain road through the Arizona Strip.

The Civilian Conservation Corps in Zion

Fulfilling his campaign promise to put a million boys to work planting trees in the national forests, Franklin D. Roosevelt launched the Civilian Conservation Corps in 1933. Though the original plan was to place 200,000 young men in 1,000 camps, by July 1933 there were 300,000 men in nearly 1,500 camps.

Horace M. Albright, Director of the National Park Service, served on the organizing committee and had the specific job of determining camp locations and outlining the work to be done. Consequently, the national parks were primary beneficiaries of this program. Camps were started in national parks, national forests, and state parks. These federal and state agencies had the responsibility of directing the work projects, while the U.S. Army operated the camps. Zion was the site of two CCC camps.

The Depression caused such severe cuts in funds to the national parks that the work of the CCC was particularly important. At Zion, the CCC constructed several buildings out of dressed stone, as well as entrance stations and signposts. Much of the park's boundary was fenced, the riverbank was stabilized, and rock curbing was installed at most parking areas. Several new trails were built, and road maintenance was an ongoing project. A few workers were privileged to assist with archaeological digs and wildlife studies.

Zion had an educational advisor for the two camps who taught popular night classes. Park rangers, project foremen, and even some enrollees served as instructors. Many young men found their careers as a result of their work or the training they received in the CCC.

World War II brought an end to the CCC, but what Zion gained from that Depression-born organization will be long lasting.

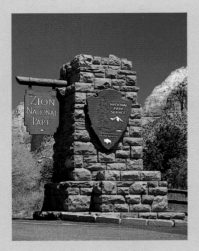

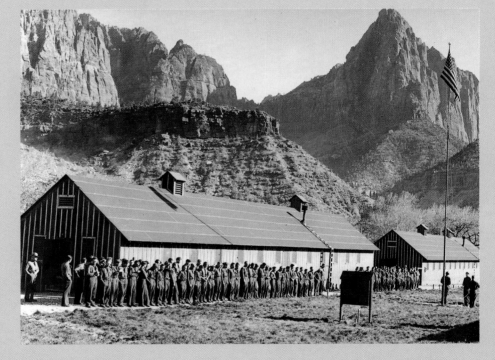

Left: Stone signposts such as this one were constructed by the CCC.
Below: The Bridge Mountain CCC camp began operating in 1933 and was the first of two camps that were established in Zion.

The Cable Story

Inconspicuously located at the beginning of the East Rim Trail at the base of Cable Mountain is a small rock pedestal. A metal plaque mounted on the pedestal tells the story of the wooden structure perched precariously 2,000 feet above. The structure is all that is left of a device that for a quarter of a century transported lumber down the mountain, and its story is a fascinating part of Zion's history.

Dave Flanigan, a young resident of Springdale, had seen a contraption consisting of wire and pulleys carry the mail up and down a mountain near Shunesburg. He thought that a similar, but heavier, machine could be built to carry lumber off the plateau into the valley below. Several years later, with the help of his brother William, Dave completed the prototype. Only gravity was used for power; the force of a loaded basket coming down propelled an empty basket up from the bottom.

The Flanigan brothers were plagued by setbacks during and after construction. Heavy loads caused runaways and overheating of the pulleys, so a braking system had to be devised.

The cable began operation on August 1, 1901, but it was four more years before Dave, William, and two

other Flanigan brothers purchased a sawmill to produce lumber to transport down the mountain. The hard work of logging as well as breakdowns, bad roads, and marketing problems had everyone discouraged.

In 1907 Dave sold the mill and the cable. The system changed hands twice more, and was never profitable for any of the owners, but it did fill a need for the Virgin River communities until better roads and transportation were available.

Left: In addition to developing the Zion Cableworks, Dave Flanigan invented a constant-velocity universal joint, a helicopter, and a windmill.
Above: The unloading platform of the Zion Cableworks in 1913.

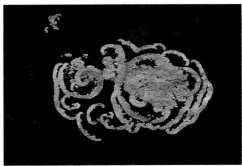

Top: Wind and water have created fluted sand-stone walls such as this throughout the park.
Above: Lichens add interesting shapes and, after rainfalls, vivid color to rock surfaces.
Left: Honeycomb weathering occurs when cavities are created in the sandstone cliffs by the dissolution of calcite, a weak cementing material that normally holds the sand grains together.

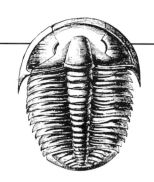

Chapter Two

GEOLOGICAL HISTORY

Zion is a geologic masterpiece. The powerful forces of nature—wind, water, faulting, and volcanic activity—created a series of rock layers that today make up the ascending series of cliffs and terraces, or "steps," of Zion's "Grand Staircase."

The history of Zion is told in its rocks. It began 240 million years ago, before the appearance of the first dinosaurs. The rocks of Zion were formed one layer above the other in orderly succession. Geologists call these layers of sedimentary rocks "formations." Each formation is unique in its composition, and each reveals the secrets of its time: the geography, climate, and the plants and animals that lived then.

There are nine distinct formations at Zion. These formations, from oldest to youngest, are the Kaibab, Moenkopi, Chinle, Moenave, Kayenta, Navajo, Temple Cap, Carmel, and Dakota. The oldest formation appears only in a few places, while the youngest appears at the top of some of Zion's tallest features.

The most important formation at Zion Canyon is the Navajo Formation. It is composed of windblown sand that has hardened into a huge mass of fine-grained sandstone. Zion owes its grandeur to this massive rock layer that forms the canyon's 2,000-foot-high vertical walls. This

formation covers a total area of approximately 150,000 square miles extending from central Wyoming to southwestern California. Wherever Navajo sandstone is exposed, streams have carved canyons into it, some of which far exceed Zion Canyon in length. Yet Zion is unique. Here the Navajo Formation reaches its maximum thickness of nearly 2,400 feet at the Temple of Sinawava. Although the top of the formation is fairly flat, forming a plateau on either side of the main canyon, erosion has created tributary valleys and side canyons, as well as a series of monolithic peaks that dominate the skyline.

An interesting characteristic of the Navajo Formation is exemplified in the Narrows, where the North Fork of the Virgin River has cut through the rock for hundreds of feet without widening the canyon. The canyon does not widen until the river channel reaches the softer layers of rock below the Navajo Formation. Where the river emerges from the Narrows at the Temple of Sinawava, the riverbed is in the Kayenta Formation and the canyon begins to widen perceptibly. The softer layers of rock allow undercutting of the cliffs which, being weakened by the thousands of vertical fractures and joints, split off, usually in long columns, leaving smooth walls above. This is

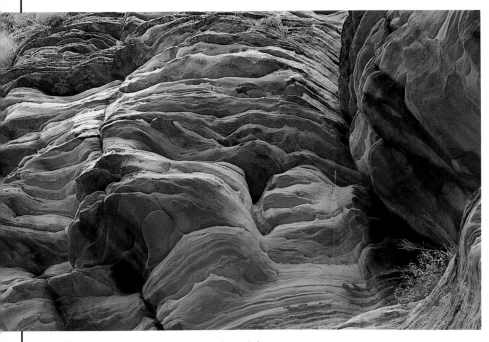

Above: Erosion and time have created myriad shapes and patterns in the sandstone.
Opposite: Golden columbine in one of Zion's many hanging gardens.

the process that keeps the walls of Zion Canyon vertical.

Another unique feature of the Navajo Formation is its exceptionally porous nature. This porosity allows water from rain and melting snow to accumulate, and as the droplets migrate downward, the rock becomes saturated. When the water reaches the more compact and impervious layer of stone contained in the Kayenta Formation, its downward path is blocked. The water then moves horizontally to the surface and emerges in the form of springs and seeps, creating Zion's famous "spring line." This phenomenon gives life to hanging gardens and creates arches and overhangs by dissolving the lime that cements the sand grains together, thus undermining and weakening the heavy rock burden above.

The spectacular, sculptured Navajo Formation is what Zion is famous for, but the other eight formations have also played a part in shaping Zion and add much to its color and charm.

The Kaibab Formation, the oldest and bottommost layer, is exposed in only two small outcrops within the park, but forms prominent cliffs west and south of the park boundary.

The Moenkopi Formation is displayed as a series of brightly colored bands, which indicate the presence of both marine and stream deposits, while the Chinle Formation consists of a solid cliff of coarse sand and gravel (Shinarump Conglomerate) covered by deposits of shale and volcanic ash that contain fossilized bones and petrified wood.

The upper part of the Moenave Formation is made up of pink, purple, and red sandstones, while the lower part consists of layers of shale. The

The Sentinel Landslide was one of many Zion-area landslides, which have left the "slump" hills that surround Springdale. Slump hills are the result of large volumes of rock or loose debris moving en masse down a slope.

presence of fish scales and skeletal parts in the bottom layers suggests that an aquatic environment characterized by lakes and sluggish streams evolved into a more terrestrial environment that had fewer, but swifter, streams.

The Kayenta Formation is made up of red and mauve siltstones and sandstones, which indicates that they were deposited by both slow and moderately flowing streams on a broad flood plain. Dinosaurs came to prominence during this period, and their tracks are still visible today, preserved in the Kayenta shale.

The Temple Cap Formation is a thin layer of heavily pigmented clay, silt, and sandstone, which is the source of the red streaking that stains the upper faces of the Navajo Formation.

The Carmel Formation is insignificant from the viewer's standpoint since it is visible only as flat-topped plateaus, but important in that it is composed primarily of fossil-bearing marine limestone, which reveals that the ocean flowed in over the desert sands and provided the calcareous cementing material found in the Navajo Formation. Also, the varying thickness of the formation (from less than a foot to 850 feet) and the pres-

ence of volcanic fragments are evidence of the beginning of crustal movement and volcanic activity.

The newest and uppermost formation, the Dakota, is visible on Horse Ranch Mountain, Zion's highest point. Here a small outcrop, consisting of tannish-colored sandstone and conglomerate, is the only evidence of this layer in the park.

The nine layers of rock at Zion tell of the many changes that have occurred over millions of years. Zion has been covered by an ocean, swept by desert winds, and has experienced earthquakes, volcanic eruptions, and landslides of gigantic proportions.

But by far the most important factor in the recent history of the formation of Zion Canyon is the Virgin River—the seemingly placid stream that continues to flow through it. Over a period of hundreds of thousands of years, water from the Virgin River and its tributary streams has moved swiftly over rock that disintegrates easily, carving the enormous canyon in the process.

The forces of nature are still at work in Zion. From a geological standpoint the canyon is young. Zion will undoubtedly look very different one million years from now, so enjoy the view while you can!

The Petrified Forest

The Petrified Forest consists of ancient trees and the remains of other formerly living things that gradually turned to stone in a geological process that took millions of years. Zion's Petrified Forest is located in the southwest corner of the park and is geologically an extension of the better-known Petrified Forest National Park in Arizona. The petrified wood found here, however, is opaque and dull colored, and not of gem quality. The hard bottom layer of the Chinle Formation consists partially of broken petrified logs, and small petrified wood fragments are found throughout the upper soft shales of the multicolored, or "painted desert" layers.

Petrified logs in the Shinarump Conglomerate of the Chinle Formation.

Just Imagine

Dinosaur tracks in the Kayenta shale of the Left Fork of North Creek.

It is easy to believe that dinosaurs existed when you look at a skeleton of one in a museum; and it is easy to visualize one traveling across the ground when you see several dinosaur tracks in the Kayenta shale of the Left Fork of North Creek. But it can be difficult to realize that the tracks are 170 million years old, and that instead of the narrow canyons and plateaus that it is today, Zion was once a vast tropical flood plain.

A visit to Zion as recently as a million years ago would have resulted in a completely different experience than a visit today. Imagine that the Great White Throne has not yet been formed, or that upon leaving the canyon you just miss getting caught by the Horse Valley landslide.

Next imagine a visit to Zion a few million years from now. The Watchman and Johnson Mountain have eroded into low red buttes. There are a few pinnacles similar to Eagle Crags where the West Temple used to be. The Great White Throne has become a conical point resembling the North Guardian Angel. A massive landslide near the Mountain of Mystery has created a lake. The Virgin River has worked its way into the Markagunt Plateau, creating a new Zion Narrows beyond State Route 14 and robbing the Sevier River of half its water. The Paiute and Sevier Bridge reservoirs are gone and agricultural land throughout central Utah has been replaced by sagebrush-covered desert.

We will never see the day, but just imagine!

MT. KINESAVA

TEMPLE CAP FORMATION

NAVAJO FORMATION

KAYENTA FORMATION

MOENAVE FORMATION

CHINLE FORMATION

PETRIFIED FOREST

TOWN OF ROCKVILLE

WEST TEMPLE

ZION CANYON

THE SENTINEL

SPRINGDALE SANDSTONE (MEMBER OF MOENAVE)

SHINARUMP CONGLOMERATE (MEMBER OF CHINLE)

MOENKOPI FORMATION

Six of Zion's layers of sedimentary rock, which are referred to as "formations," can be seen in this panoramic view from near Smithsonian Butte. Zion's two youngest formations, the Dakota and the Carmel, are not visible here, nor is the Kaibab, Zion's oldest formation. The Springdale Sandstone and the Shinarump Conglomerate are part of the Moenave and Chinle formations, respectively.

Chapter Three

FLORA AND FAUNA

Zion is home to a wide variety of plant and animal life. A wide range of elevations, shaded canyons, and open, sunny slopes create environmental extremes from moist forests to rugged deserts. Plants and animals suited to these diverse conditions have evolved over time and live side by side in a delicate ecological balance.

MAMMALS

Nearly everyone who visits the park sees some of Zion's 68 species of mammals, 36 species of reptiles, 7 species of amphibians, and 271 species of birds.

The mule deer is found throughout the area and is the largest mammal one is likely to see in the park. A few elk reside in the higher Kolob Plateau to the north, but generally they prefer more open country than the park provides. The desert bighorn sheep is native to the area but disappeared prior to 1950. Though it has been reintroduced, it is seldom seen.

Predators include the mountain lion (also commonly called the cougar), bobcat, coyote, gray fox, badger, and the weasel. The one known shrew is classed as an insectivore, along with several species of bats.

The wolf and otter have long since left Zion. The raccoon was once numerous, but disappeared during the 1920s. Should you be driving through the canyon at night, you might spot a relative of the raccoon— the ringtail cat. This handsome creature is nocturnal and may raid your camp looking for food.

Of the many rodents in the park, the most obvious is the gray rock squirrel, which is sometimes a nuisance to campers. The little antelope ground squirrel is less numerous but more likely to be seen year-round. You may never catch a glimpse of the pocket gopher, but its mounds are present at all elevations. Likewise, the presence of the wood rat, or pack rat, is evidenced by the many "trash piles" this nighttime raider builds

Page 22–23: A brilliantly colored stand of aspen in Kolob Canyons.
Page 22–23 insets from left to right: The badger is one of Zion's common predators; the notoriously bold Steller's jay resides primarily in coniferous forests; the beaver species found in Zion does not build dams, but rather lives in burrows along the banks of the Virgin River.
Previous page top: The collared lizard is one of the more colorful reptiles found in Zion.
Previous page bottom: Fallen leaves herald the coming of winter for Zion's wildlife.
Above: The short-horned lizard is active during daytime hours and feeds on ants and other insects.
Top right: Though ferocious looking, the tarantula is relatively harmless.

around the entrances to its dens.

The porcupine is also found in the park, but is more numerous on the plateau than in the canyon. The beaver was absent from the park for 50 years, but reappeared in about 1940 while migrating up the Virgin River from the Colorado River. It is called a "bank beaver" since it lives in burrows and generally does not build dams. The cottontail and jackrabbit are found in the park, but the jackrabbit seldom ventures into the canyon.

REPTILES AND AMPHIBIANS

Nonvenomous reptiles and amphibians make up an interesting part of Zion's fauna. The most visible among these are lizards, the largest being the vegetarian chuckwalla, which may reach a length of 20 inches. The most colorful lizards are the hardest to see because they are less common and well camouflaged. These include the collared lizard, banded gecko, and western skink. The whiptail may also be colorful and is numerous. It has a long, slender, striped body, and the tails of the young range in color from blue to green. The two species of horned lizard are the desert horned lizard, which is nearly always seen below 5,500 feet, and the short-horned

lizard, which stays above 6,000 feet.

Like the horned lizards, some of Zion's snakes have a narrow habitat range. For example, the black-and-white–banded common kingsnake is seldom, if ever, found above 4,500 feet, and its more colorful relative, the Sonoran Mountain kingsnake, has never been seen below 6,500 feet. This species is quite rare and is often persecuted because of its resemblance to the venomous coral snake. Note that there are no coral snakes in Zion.

The western rattler is a venomous snake that may be found at all elevations up to 8,000 feet. Though it may appear threatening if startled or cornered, it will usually retreat rather than strike. Its venom is not as virulent as that of some other snake species, but it can be deadly, nevertheless.

BIRDS

About 271 bird species have been recorded in Zion. Of this number, approximately 60 are permanent residents and over 100 are known to breed in the area, including three species of hummingbirds, the golden eagle, and the rare peregrine falcon. The song birds include the robin, black-headed grosbeak, lazuli bunting, Townsend's solitaire, and both

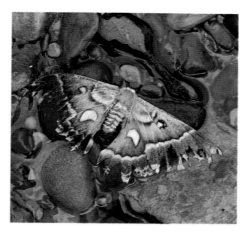

*Clockwise from top left: This hornet's nest
appears to be growing out of rock; a moth resting
on similarly colored rock; the common raven is an
opportunistic and omnivorous feeder, and includes
carrion in its diet; the mule deer is the largest
mammal you are likely to see in the park.*

the solitary and warbling vireo. The
canyon wren's song—a clear, sweet
cascade of descending notes—can be
heard any month of the year. The
ungainly, soot-colored dipper has a
surprisingly pretty song, and it usually sings to the accompaniment of a
babbling brook or stream where it
dives for food. The dipper may build
its nest in a hanging garden where it
is hidden underneath a projection of
dripping tufa (porous rock) and vegetation. Other choice nesting sites are
behind waterfalls and in damp caves.

Seven members of the crow family
are found in Zion, three of which
nest here. The raven and scrub jay
are ever present and the Steller's jay
frequents the canyon from its normal range in the higher elevations.
With the exception of the rare gray
jay, these are the noisiest birds in the
park. The call of the gregarious
pinyon jay always precedes its arrival.
This species is sometimes called the
"blue crow." It appears in great flocks
throughout the pinyon-juniper belt.
The raven is a notorious clown and
bully, and delights in making life
miserable for the soaring hawks and
eagles, whom it dive-bombs repeat-
edly. The raven usually wins these
encounters.

The roadrunner, a member of the
cuckoo family, is also considered a
clown by some. Its methods of loco-
motion and obtaining food may appear comical, but the roadrunner is
deadly serious when it flails a rattlesnake to death and swallows it whole.
The roadrunner is a desert dweller,
but has been observed among the
aspen trees in late summer at an
elevation of 9,000 feet.

ANIMALS AND YOUR SAFETY

No wild animal is a threat to humans as long as it is treated as a wild creature and not as a pet. Even a seemingly tame deer can inflict a wound with a hoof or antler, and a friendly looking squirrel can cause a deep bite with its teeth. DO NOT FEED ANIMALS IN THE PARK. IT IS ILLEGAL AND THEY WILL HURT YOU!

One potentially harmful animal that hikers often ask about is the mountain lion. Attacks by mountain lions on humans are very rare, and they are not a reason for concern during your visit to Zion. Fortunate indeed is the visitor who catches sight of a mountain lion, as most residents of the area never do, although their tracks are ever present, especially in the Kolob district. If you should meet a mountain lion, give it an opportunity to leave. However, it is more likely that the animal will spot you first and retreat.

Just a word of warning in case you should find a fox that appears tame or sick, or a bat that appears disoriented, DO NOT TOUCH! These animals are known to carry rabies and should be reported to the rangers.

The tarantula is a large, hairy spider that comes out of hiding in late summer and fall to look for a mate. This species has been severely persecuted as it was thought to be deadly. But the fact is that it is relatively harmless. Its bite may be painful, but is not life threatening. Let the tarantula live; it consumes many annoying insect pests.

Do not kill snakes. If a rattlesnake is near your camp, have a ranger remove it. Learn to distinguish between rattlesnakes and gopher snakes. Gopher snakes are the largest of Zion's reptiles, and may attain a length of six feet. They will not harm you but should be left alone as should all wildlife.

Left: Mule deer.
Right: The porcupine is frequently found in higher elevations.

Z I O N

The Virgin River

Zion Canyon was carved and shaped by the Virgin River, a tributary of the Colorado River, which is nine times as long and 50 times larger by volume, but has only one-seventh the gradient. Two main branches make up the Virgin River: the North Fork (Mukuntuweap), which originates as springs north of Zion's north boundary at an elevation of 9,000 feet, and the East Fork (Parunuweap), which originates in similar highlands east of the North Fork and drains Long Valley, which runs along Highway 89. The Virgin River is about 160 miles long and empties into Lake Mead, some 25 miles short of the original Colorado River channel. There is a total drop of 7,800 feet in elevation along the Virgin River, for an average of 48 feet per mile. This gradient increases to 76 feet per mile through Zion Canyon.

Where the North Fork passes the park headquarters, the average flow is 100 cubic feet per second. However, the river has been known to slow to 20 cubic feet per second following several dry years. Although the stream may appear quite clear much of the time, it is actually full of fine, suspended silt; enough in fact to fill 30 dump trucks (120 cubic yards) in a 24-hour period. It is estimated that a flood of 10 times the normal flow carries 2,000 times as much solid material. One hour of flooding removes more silt, sand, and gravel than one year of normal flow. In addition to the usual month or more of runoff from melting snow in the spring, floods may occur many times a year. This makes it easy to understand how the little Virgin River could carry so many cubic miles of earth over the eons and play a major role in shaping Zion Canyon.

Opposite: Zion's side canyons are replete with moss-lined waterfalls such as this one. Clockwise from top: Showy goldeneye; claret cup cactus; hoary aster; shooting star.

PLANT LIFE

A great variety of plants thrive in Zion. Shady side canyons, a wide range of elevations, and disparate sources of water provide diverse environments for biotic communities. Consequently, plants requiring very little water cover desert hills and live only a short distance from the lush greenery that grows along the banks of the Virgin River.

The most noticeable plant community below 5,000 feet is composed of pinyon and juniper, two evergreen species that grow together in an association known throughout the West as the "pygmy forest." It dominates the talus slopes and sandy benches below the vertical cliffs of Zion. Scattered among these evergreen species are serviceberry, single-leaf ash, roundleaf buffaloberry, manzanita, joint fir, cliffrose, and various types of cacti. Gambel oak, scrub live oak, and bigtooth maple also appear in patches.

Also found in the canyon is the riparian woodland, a narrow band of deciduous trees that grow along the river and its tributaries. The Fremont cottonwood is dominant, and is the largest of the riverbank varieties, followed by the box elder and velvet ash. Several types of willow are also common. Water birch occurs primarily in the very wet areas in side canyons. The ground cover in this community has undergone considerable change since the occupation of the canyon. Where sandbar willows and wild roses used to dominate, the exotic tamarisk, or salt cedar, has largely taken over and forms dense thickets in many places.

The terraces and plateaus from 5,500 to 7,500 feet are characterized by ponderosa pine (the largest of local conifers), Rocky Mountain juniper, and sagebrush. Gambel oak is also prominent at this elevation. Douglas fir and white fir are also fairly abundant, although they usually live, along with the quaking

Left: A lone yucca stands alongside a weathered and dying ponderosa pine. Above: Detail of a prickly pear cactus. Right: Beavertail cactus.

aspens, at higher elevations. The 14 varieties of cacti that have been identified in Zion are divided into three groups commonly called hedgehog, cholla (tree cactus), and prickly pear. Identification, especially between the prickly pears and chollas, is difficult and confusing because they hybridize so readily. The most colorful, if not the most abundant, of Zion's wildflowers belong to the cactus family. The claret cup, smallest of the hedgehogs, is the first to bloom. It sometimes blooms as early as March, followed by its larger relative, the purple torch. Some varieties of cacti may bloom as late as August, but you will find the most profuse display in May and June.

Two species of yuccas grow in Zion. One, the narrowleaf, or Spanish bayonet, produces a flower stalk of white blossoms reaching several feet above the spines, inspiring its popu-

lar name, Lord's Candlestick. The yuccas, which belong to the lily family, are erroneously called cacti by some and, along with the cacti, are considered "desert" plants. Zion is a desert canyon, and has an average annual rainfall of about 15 inches, so both cacti and yuccas are perfectly at home throughout the park, even up to 7,500 feet in areas with southern exposure.

If the desert plants seem out of place on the plateau tops, likewise, several mountain varieties are found at the bottom of the canyon in areas of limited sunlight and only adequate moisture. In Emerald Pools Canyon, for instance, entirely different plants grow on opposite sides of the canyon, though the canyon walls are only a few hundred feet apart. At the end of the Gateway to the Narrows Trail, a yucca grows on a cliff ledge just a few yards directly above a

Douglas fir tree. Hanging gardens are found at several places where water seeps constantly from the vertical rock walls, depositing calcareous tufa, which gives footing and life to a variety of water-loving plants. The two most accessible hanging gardens are at Weeping Rock and along the Gateway to the Narrows Trail. In addition to grasses and banks of maidenhair ferns, such flowers as golden columbine, shooting star, purple violet, and cardinal monkey flower grow abundantly. The latter species blooms in spring and again in September. Scarlet lobelia, or cardinal-flower, while not a part of the hanging garden, may be found nearby in late summer.

From the east end of the Zion tun-

Left: Ponderosa pines silhouetted against the evening sky. Above: Needle clusters from a ponderosa pine.

nel to the East Entrance to the park, the Zion–Mt. Carmel Highway winds about eight miles through cuts and around contours in the upper half of the massive Navajo Formation. On these sandstone slopes, ponderosa pine, littleleaf mountain mahogany, Douglas fir, and Rocky Mountain juniper appear to be growing out of solid rock. As this side canyon widens into a sandy valley bottom near the East Entrance, ponderosa pine and juniper are joined by Gambel oak, sagebrush, manzanita, and joint fir. Manzanita and joint fir are also found, though in fewer numbers, on the rocky slopes and sandy benches of the main canyon.

It seems odd that the first blossoms of spring may appear on the higher slopes instead of in the lower elevations. The tiny pink Japanese-lanternlike blossoms of the manzanita usually begin to appear in January, but have been known to bloom in December at an elevation of 6,000 feet. The low-growing sand buttercup blooms in March, or earlier, in the sandy areas near the east end of the tunnel. Small, brilliant, orange-scarlet clumps of slickrock paintbrush dot the slopes. Look for purplish blue spiderwort along the roadsides and other sandy areas. Red and purple penstemons bloom along the roadsides throughout the summer, but the last flower to bloom in this section of the park is the bright red hummingbird trumpet, which looks like penstemon but be-

longs to the evening primrose family.

Perhaps displaying the best color of all is the bigtooth maple, which turns brilliant shades of red before dropping its leaves in October. It grows along the streambed of Clear Creek, the drainage that the road follows through the slickrock area east of the tunnel.

A few species catch everyone's eyes, depending on the time of year. For a short period in early spring, the disturbed areas on the canyon floor become solid purple from the bloom of the foul-smelling member of the mustard family, *Chorispora tenella,* which seems to have been introduced within the last two decades and has no common name. Desert beauty, also known as "purple sage," is a blooming shrub that belongs to the pea family. The true purple sage blossoms earlier and is very conspicuous on the hills near the Zion

Canyon Visitor Center for only a few days. The tall yellow spikes of another mustard, the prince's plume, has a wide distribution on the rocky slopes, and retains some of its blossoms throughout the summer. Perhaps the biggest attention-getter in the park is the sacred datura, a member of the nightshade family, which may have as many as a hundred large, white, funnel-shaped flowers. The blossoms open at night and usually close by midday. This plant is so abundant in the park that it has been given the nickname "Zion lily."

A small tree that is not widely distributed and could go unnoticed except when it is in bloom is the New Mexico locust. When it blooms, the aroma is intoxicating. Best seen along the road near Weeping Rock and near the west door of the Zion Canyon Visitor Center, the New Mexico locust's clusters of pink flowers bloom a second time if summer showers are abundant.

Top left to right: Riverbank grass; manzanita; maidenhair fern; sacred datura, or "Zion lily." Bottom: A ponderosa pine appears to be growing out of solid rock.

Chapter Four

LANDMARKS

Zion's dramatic landscape is filled with many remarkable geologic features. Its jutting rocks, high plateaus, broad mesas, towering cliffs, and deep canyons form breathtaking scenic vistas that thrill the visitor. Certain features are so extraordinary that they are considered landmarks. Long before the establishment of Zion as a national park, these natural formations served to guide the way for pioneers and visitors. Names such as the Great White Throne, the Temple of Sinawava, and the Towers of the Virgin reflect the exalted emotions people felt when they looked upon these monumental works of nature—highlights in a natural landscape where the spectacular is commonplace.

RIVERSIDE WALK

The Riverside Walk is the easiest and most popular of Zion's trails. The paved section of the trail begins where the scenic drive ends at the Temple of Sinawava. It parallels the river for one mile, and ends at the point where the canyon narrows significantly, requiring hikers to take to the water.

A canopied interpretive facility is located at the trailhead, and interpretive signs are placed along the way. A hard-surfaced trail with very little incline, the Riverside Walk is suitable for people in wheelchairs (with assistance) and children in strollers. Naturalist-guided walks provide an opportunity to see the many interesting features along the way. Among the highlights is a desert swamp that contains typical water-growing plants, leopard frogs, and a spring with a constant temperature of 70 degrees Fahrenheit, plus or minus one degree. You will also see the Stadium with its arched canyon walls, and may hear the goatlike call of the canyon tree frog. The most luxuriant of Zion's hanging gardens are here; and living among the many flowering plants is the Zion snail, found nowhere else in the world. Dark brown to black in color, full-size snails are only about one-eighth of an inch in diameter. Birds become less noticeable as the canyon narrows, but look for the dipper, black phoebe, canyon wren, and the winter wren.

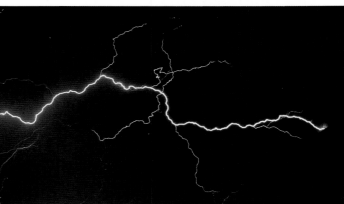

The view of the Mountain of Mystery at the end of the trail is spectacular, but if the river is higher than usual, viewing the sight may require getting your feet wet.

THE EAST & WEST TEMPLES

While the Great White Throne has become, to many, the symbol of Zion, the West Temple is the beacon. Early travelers used it as a guide since it could be seen from afar from several different directions. The West Temple dominates the landscape with its location, height, and distinctive symmetry, which set it apart from its otherwise homogeneous companions, the Towers of the Virgin.

In 1903 the West Temple was described by Frederick S. Dellenbaugh as a "Titanic mountain of bare rock" that "lift[ed] its opalescent shoulders alluringly against the eastern sky."

The West Temple is located near the southwest corner of the park, and is the highest point on the canyon wall. As viewed from the Zion Canyon Visitor Center, the West Temple and Altar of Sacrifice, including several pinnacles in between, form the headwall of Oak Creek Canyon, and are part of what has been called the greatest skyline in the world.

The East Temple, on the opposite side of the canyon, is less imposing, being about 700 feet lower than the West Temple. It, too, is crowned by the red Temple Cap Formation, which gives the East and West Temples a terraced, or decklike, appearance.

The Temple Cap Formation appears in several other peaks, and while it is not especially noticeable on the Altar of Sacrifice, a remnant of it provides the red color from which this feature gets its name.

Moonsets, lightning storms, stream channels cutting through rock faces, and frozen waterfalls create a variety of moods.

KOLOB CANYONS

The Kolob Canyons section of the park, located in Zion's northwest corner, has an appeal and grandeur all its own. Kolob's Finger Canyons are as dramatic and awe-inspiring as any sight in Zion. To get to them, take Exit 40 from Interstate 15, about 18 miles south of Cedar City and 27 miles north of St. George.

A 5.2-mile-long spur road leads alongside Taylor Creek, over Lee Pass, and into the Timber Creek drainage. It is here that one sees an entirely different Zion. Looming to the left are the fingers of the Navajo Formation, with narrow, 1,600-foot-deep canyons in between. In Kolob Canyons the Navajo Formation is red, or salmon colored, all the way to the top.

The sharp eastward dip of the strata reveals secrets of Zion's past. Two geologic events, about one hundred million years apart, were largely responsible for shaping this part of the park. The first was the compression of the earth's crust, which caused a north-south fold in the stratified rock, called an anticline. The anticline is named the Kanarra Fold. The second event was the Hurricane Fault. A crack in the earth split Kanarra Fold along its axis, pushing the east side upward much higher than the west side. Subsequent ero-

sion has resulted in further exposure of this fault.

One of Kolob Canyons' most impressive sights is the magnificent Kolob Arch, whose 310-foot span makes it possibly the largest free-standing arch in the world. Visitors who take the 14-mile round-trip hike to Kolob Arch are treated to a spectacular view of the arch from the canyon floor.

SLICKROCK

The Slickrock area of Zion has no definite boundaries—even the name is unofficial—but it is generally considered to encompass the area between the tunnel and the East Entrance to the park. This eight-mile section of the park must resemble, except for the green trees and shrubs, the vast desert of sand dunes that it was 140 million years ago.

The term "slickrock" was probably coined by a local rancher who watched one of his animals fall to its doom (as frequently happened on the original East Rim Trail). But the name of this rock formation is a misnomer because it is not slick at all. In fact, the sandstone that bears the name is actually quite rough to the touch, but loose grains of sand make it slippery.

The upper half of the Navajo Formation weathers and erodes quite readily, and many domes and slopes

develop varying degrees of steepness. Such areas support very little vegetation, but they add to the variety and beauty of the scenery. Only a flight over the park or a hike in the back-country will reveal the extent to which this sandstone is found in Zion.

EMERALD POOLS

In a short canyon opposite Zion Lodge, pools have been formed by the gouging action of two waterfalls. One of the pools is at the base of a precipitous canyon wall that is part of the Navajo Formation, and the other is below a lesser cliff. Though officially named Heaps Canyon, this area is usually referred to as Emerald

Opposite: Kolob Arch is one of Zion's most impressive sights.
Left: An autumn view from Highway 14 south toward Zion National Park.
Above: Backlit waterfall at Emerald Pools.
Below left: Bigtooth maple leaves turn brilliant shades of red before they fall.
Below right: Plains prickly pear cactus.

Above: The Great White Throne.
Right: Waterfall at the Lower Pool.

Pools, a name resulting from the green tinge that algae has given the water.

A paved path, which accommodates people in wheelchairs and children in strollers, leads six-tenths of a mile to the Lower Pool through groves of oak, maple, ash, Rocky Mountain juniper, and fir. A trail beyond the paved path leads behind the waterfall and beneath an overhanging cliff where the seeping water deposits tufa (calcium carbonate, or limestone) and gives life to the hanging gardens. Minnows and dippers may be observed in the pool below.

A half-mile ungraded trail takes you to the Upper Pool, which is also small, but deeper than the Lower Pool. The canyon wren and the diminutive winter wren can be seen darting in and out of the crevices. The cardinal-flower blooms here in late summer.

Just on top of the cliff above the Lower Pool is yet another pool, which is hardly deep enough to wet your ankles. It is a favorite of photographers for catching reflections of the cliffs. Take care to stay well back from the edge of the cliff.

THE GREAT WHITE THRONE

Looming 2,000 feet above the river, the Great White Throne is probably the best display of the Navajo Formation anywhere.

Only the top half of the Great White Throne is white, but even that may not appear so without the reflection of the late afternoon sunlight. Mosses, lichens, and mineral stains alter or conceal much of the natural color of the rock.

The back side of this peak was first scaled in 1929 by Bill Evans, a Californian who made a solo climb to the summit. He fell on the way down but was rescued by rangers and recovered completely.

Paintings of the Great White Throne have hung in railroad depots across the nation, and a stamp bearing a picture of it was issued in 1934.

Z I O N

Pine Creek Bridge

The arch bridge that spans Pine Creek was completed in 1930, just in time for the tunnel dedication on July 4. This impressive, man-made structure was the brainchild of Harry Langley, a National Park Service landscape architect.

Langley wanted the bridge to be made of local stone to blend in with the natural colors of its surroundings. He built a miniature out of green laundry soap first, meticulously carving each piece with a pocket knife. Using the miniature as a guide, workmen cut a sheet-metal template for each stone in the face of the bridge.

The Reynolds-Ely Company, the primary contractor on the Mt. Carmel section of the road, also held the contract to build the Pine Creek Bridge. Lou Whitney, a bridge builder from Springville, Utah, had built bridges and culverts in other areas of the park before becoming supervisor of the Pine Creek Bridge project. He carried out Langley's mandate that every color of rock found in the cliffs of Zion be incorporated into the structure.

Therefore, instead of simply quarrying for rock in a single location, it was gathered from many sections of the canyon. The huge boulders that had rolled to the canyon floor from the Moenave and lower Navajo formations were the principal source of rock for the bridge. More than 50 men worked to quarry, transport, dress, and lay the stone. Since the completion of the project, time, weathering, and lichen growth have all contributed to further the "natural" appearance of a bridge that is truly in harmony with its surroundings.

Park visitors can decide for themselves whether or not the architect achieved his goal of incorporating all of Zion's colors into this unique bridge.

Above: A misty curtain of water at Weeping Rock.
Top right: Fall maples and a cottonwood near the Temple of Sinawava.
Far right: Icicles on a weeping rock.

TEMPLE OF SINAWAVA

Seven miles from the South Entrance, the scenic drive terminates in a giant rotunda with the sky as its dome. A remnant of a Navajo Formation wall projecting into the canyon is now eroded and resembles a fin. This serrated rock wall ends in a slender column about 150 feet high, which is named the Pulpit. Although the canyon is not a box canyon (one having no outlets), the closeness of the walls helps give the illusion of one. The other part of the wall is called the Altar. The Temple of Sinawava is the area surrounded by 2,000-foot-high perpendicular cliffs. From a narrow hanging valley on the west wall, one of Zion Canyon's most spectacular waterfalls drops nearly 1,000 feet, provided it is raining or snow is melting on the West Rim.

The Temple of Sinawava is a good place to watch the busy dipper along the river and listen for the songs of other birds such as the black-headed grosbeak, solitary vireo, or canyon wren.

The Temple of Sinawava is the head of the Riverside Walk and the termination of the top to-bottom Narrows hike. An interpretive display, a restroom, and a drinking fountain are provided for the convenience of visitors.

Looking down the canyon, one can easily recognize the Great White Throne and Angels Landing. Observation Point is the white-topped formation on the left.

WEEPING ROCK

Weeping Rock is one of Zion's genuine novelties. From a parking area near the base of Cable Mountain, it is a quick quarter-mile walk up to Weeping Rock, an area that best illustrates the Zion "spring line." The perpetual "weeping" of the rock is caused by water that seeps down from Echo Canyon, a hanging (secondary) valley whose floor is higher than that of the main valley.

The downward movement of the water is blocked at Weeping Rock by an impervious layer of rock, forcing it to move horizontally to the surface where it oozes from several hundred square feet of vertical cliff face. The "spring line" is the intersection between the porous and nonporous rock where water is forced to the surface of the rock. Nourished by the water, hanging gardens grow out of the rock on the cliff face.

The self-guided nature trail leading uphill to Weeping Rock should be taken at a leisurely pace so that you can read the small interpretive signs placed at intervals. Freezing temperatures may force the closure of this trail for several weeks during winter because of the giant icicles that form, creating a hazard for anyone walking directly below. This trail is also a good location from which to observe a variety of Zion's feathered fauna. The brushy hillside above the parking area is a favorite nesting site of the blue-gray gnatcatcher, and the dipper and winter wren have been observed along Weeping Rock Creek. The high-pitched chatter of the white-throated swift is a common sound in summer, issuing from high overhead. The rare peregrine falcon, one of the world's fastest-flying birds, is known sometimes to nest in this vicinity.

Z I O N

Volcanoes

Though the two most frequently visited areas of the park—Zion Canyon and Kolob Canyons—show little evidence of volcanic activity, Zion actually has numerous volcanic deposits. They are concentrated chiefly along the western boundary, which is also the location of minor faults. This, of course, suggests a relationship between the faults and the volcanoes. However, the volcanic eruptions that deposited what we see today took place long after the crustal movements occurred, and after the land acquired its present profile. Zion's volcanoes were formed within the last two million years, which is quite recent in geological terms. Evidence of the eruptions is visible along the Kolob Reservoir Road to Lava Point.

CHECKERBOARD MESA

Checkerboard Mesa is the first of Zion's features the visitor encounters upon entering the park at the East Entrance. This symmetrical formation appears as a truncated cone, and is carved into the upper, white portion of the Navajo Formation. It exhibits a surface pattern of imperfect horizontal and vertical lines that resembles a giant fish net laid out to dry. This particular design (called "checkerboarding" here at Zion) occurs only on a few other peaks within the park, and always on the north-facing, shaded side of the peak, indicating a relationship with climatic conditions characterized by prolonged periods of exposure to snow and ice.

Horizontal lines in rock are found in other places in the park, and are common wherever Navajo sandstone is exposed. They are caused by differential erosion along horizontal bedding planes. The rate of erosion is controlled by the varying degree of coarseness of sand particles and the concentration of cementing material (principally calcite) and its solubility.

The less common vertical lines (which are not to be confused with jointing, a regular feature of Navajo sandstone) are of special interest, partly because of their rarity. They are found only on the surface of the rock, and are thought to originate as shallow cracks caused by the expansion and contraction that occurs during the freezing and thawing processes. Subsequent enlargement is caused by runoff from rain and melting snow.

THE KOLOB RESERVOIR ROAD TO LAVA POINT

The Kolob Reservoir Road is a fascinating but too often overlooked part of Zion. Beginning at the town of Virgin, 15 miles west of the South Entrance, the road runs north from there and gains 4,400 feet in elevation in 16 miles. Its ultimate destination is Lava Point, a fire lookout station located at 7,900 feet that has a view of the canyon and much of the plateau. A primitive campground is maintained nearby and several trails

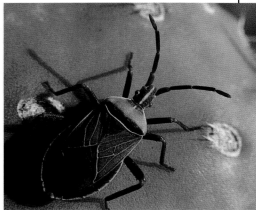

and off-trail hikes start there.

Originally a pioneer ranch road, it is now both a scenic drive and a thoroughfare for local ranchers. Some outstanding features to look for on the ascent are Tabernacle Dome, Burnt Mountain, Timber Top, Jobs Head, and the North and South Guardian Angels. Jobs Head is part of the Navajo Formation and is located between Firepit Knoll and Maloney Hill. Its most significant feature is the point where the formation's color turns from white to red.

After leaving Virgin, the road

follows North Creek for a short distance along the base of a ridge, which is capped by a layer of basalt (volcanic rock occurring in sheetlike lava flows) that is a million years old. The layer to the right was laid down in an ancient valley bottom during a volcanic eruption, forcing a once-flowing stream to find a new route. The ridge ahead, above the Sunset Canyon Ranch, illustrates that this phenomenon occurred again one quarter of a million years ago. The road rises 2,300 feet in five and a half miles where a now-hardened

Top left: Checkerboard Mesa.
Top right: Ponderosa pine seedling.
Above: Beetle commonly found on prickly pear cacti.
Far left: Distant view of West Temple from Cave Valley on the Kolob Reservoir Road.

Hikers on the Hop Valley Trail may encounter cattle on the privately owned property along the way.

lava flow once blocked North Creek (on the east side) and intermittent drainages (on the west side) and caused them to incise new passages (that eventually became canyons) into the softer sedimentary layers. The road levels out for a short distance in Cave Valley, where sand from eroding cliffs in the Navajo Formation covers the underlying basalt.

The road climbs again and passes Spendlove and Firepit Knolls, which are two cinder cones that lie on the East Cougar Mountain Fault, and mark the last episodes of volcanic activity in Zion. Firepit Knoll, north of the road, is red instead of black like most volcanic craters. To the south, Lee Valley has developed along the East Cougar Mountain Fault, and is partially filled with basalt. After crossing the head of Lee Valley, the road ascends Maloney Hill where still another, and much older (1.4 million years), hardened lava flow drapes over a sandstone cliff in the Navajo Formation. Immediately to the west

is Jobs Head, the point at which the Navajo Formation changes from white to red. The road ascends further through the lava and sandstone buttes of the Navajo and Temple Cap formations until it reaches the shale that is characteristic of the Carmel Formation. Home Valley Knoll, another basaltic cinder cone, appears to the right of the road near the turnoff to Lava Point. It is thought to be the source of the thick layer of basalt that constitutes Lava Point.

The last three and a half miles of the road to Lava Point are not paved. Though there are other roads leading down the mountain, they are steep and dusty. Visitors should obtain information at one of the visitor centers regarding weather and road conditions.

From Lava Point, you have a panoramic view of Zion Canyon and can see the gray and pink layers of rock to the east and north. On a clear day, Mt. Trumbull, near the North Rim of the Grand Canyon, is also visible.

ZION

Who Named What

Zion Canyon was named by its first Mormon settler, a farmer named Isaac Behunin. One evening while sitting on his front porch in the lingering twilight, he gazed across the canyon. He was so moved by its grandeur that it inspired him to recall a passage in the Bible (Isa. 2:2-3) that mentions a place called Zion, found "in the top of the mountains," where "the Lord's house shall be established." Behunin felt that he had discovered such a place, and from that moment on, he called it Zion.

Many of the names for individual features within the park were given by park officials, and the logic behind most choices is obvious. One red peak with an arch became Red Arch Mountain, and another became Lady Mountain when someone saw in it the likeness of a woman.

Johnson Mountain was named for the canyon's discoverer, Nephi Johnson. A visiting Methodist minister, Frederick Fisher, and two of his friends were responsible for labeling the Three Patriarchs, the Great White Throne, and Angels Landing. Other features were designated by topographers and scientists, or named after local residents.

Chapter Five

PRESERVATION

The idea of earth as a paradise, as a place to be cherished for its bounty, was a view contrary to the pioneer way of thinking. To many, the vast American West was an inhospitable wilderness to be subdued. But others recognized that, for all its wildness, this was an unspoiled land where the native people existed in harmony with nature.

George Catlin, the noted painter of Native American life, was concerned that the westward expansion was threatening the natural state of indigenous cultures, wildlife, and wilderness. In 1832, Catlin became the first to propose the idea of the government's preserving "a magnificent park . . . A nation's park, containing man and beast, in all wildness and freshness of their nature's beauty!"

More than 150 years later, Catlin's message of conservation is still timely. Because of the steady increase in visitation during the last decade, many national parks have sustained damage to once pristine natural habitats. With its annual visitation currently exceeding 2.5 million, Zion National Park has not been spared the consequences of overcrowding.

The natural beauty of Zion is quickly being altered by the very people for whose enjoyment it was created. Traffic, trash, and graffiti are the most noticeable signs of overcrowding and

abuse. While such symptoms are unsightly and detract from the natural beauty of the park, they have a much more serious and far-reaching impact on vegetation and wildlife.

Zion National Park is home to a variety of plant and animal species. Among these are a number of locally rare and threatened and endangered species, including the Gambel's quail, desert bighorn sheep, peregrine falcon, and Mexican spotted owl. Historically, Zion has been a refuge for all native wildlife, but the increase in visitation has brought with it changes that are altering the animals' habitat. The presence of humans not only affects animals in what is left behind—trash and grafitti, for example—but also in what illegally leaves with them, such as indigenous rocks and plants.

Although Zion is protected from development and private ownership,

Pages 48–49: Canyon hiking in Zion.
Previous page top: Rare Gambel's quail.
Previous page bottom: Bigtooth maple.
Top: Rare desert bighorn sheep.
Middle: The National Park Service helps to make
visiting Zion more enjoyable.
Bottom: Traffic congestion in Zion Canyon is
taking its toll on the environment.
Opposite: Yucca plants in Kolob Canyons.

the park does not exist in a vacuum. It must be protected from within park boundaries as well. The National Park Service has recognized the problems that come with overcrowding and is doing its part to conserve the scenery and the natural and historic objects and wildlife. The park service is also working to provide for visitors' enjoyment of them in a manner that will leave them unimpaired for the enjoyment of future generations.

New solutions include restricting parking in Zion Canyon and implementing a shuttle-bus system, and educating visitors about the types of problems that come with too many people wanting to be in the same place at once. By showing respect and consideration for the park and the plant and animal life that make their home here, the uniqueness of Zion can be preserved for future generations. However, this can be done only with the help of each and every visitor. The role of people in wilderness is one of balancing enjoyment with the need for preservation.

Top: Trees in autumn color, Pine Creek.
Bottom: Hikers are encouraged to leave no trace of
their presence in the park. This includes staying
on designated trails and carrying out all trash.
Pages 54–55: Winter solstice snowfall on the
Virgin River, Zion Canyon.

WHAT YOU CAN DO TO HELP

To keep Zion National Park recognized and valued worldwide as an outstanding example of balance between preservation and use:

■ Put all litter in trash cans. When hiking, carry a trash bag with you and collect any litter you may encounter.

■ Observe wildlife from a distance—never feed the animals, doing so can endanger them and you.

■ Show respect for the plants and animals—you are a visitor in their home.

■ Please drive safely. Take your time; park roads are not designed for speed.

■ Stay on designated trails.

■ Speak out if you see careless or destructive acts in progress. Report details of incidents to a park ranger.

■ If you value the national park system, call or write your elected representatives. Your voice needs to be heard.

Your vision for how Zion should look to future generations is important to the National Park Service. If you have any comments or questions, please write to:

Superintendent
Zion National Park
Springdale, Utah 84767-1099

Prehistoric Rock Art

One of the more enduring archeological features in Zion is Native American rock art. The term *rock art* refers to both petroglyphs, which are drawings and symbols carved in stone, and pictographs, which are images painted on stone.

The rock art in southwestern Utah is the work of the Anasazi people who inhabited the area for a thousand years from A.D. 200 to about 1250. The Kaibab Paiute, who have lived in the area for the last eight hundred years, also created rock art. There are many more prehistoric sites in Zion than previously thought. An excellent petroglyph site lies just off the East Entrance approach road.

The park service is working to enhance public appreciation of archeological remains. Although there is a great deal of controversy about the meaning of rock art, one thing is certain: the art represents a cultural legacy and needs our protection.

Visitors should view all rock art without touching because the oils and acids on our fingers will damage rock art. All rock art on both state and federal land is protected. People who vandalize or remove rock art are subject to severe penalties under the Archeological Resources Protection Act of 1979.

The rock art of Zion is all that is left of a people whose way of life has vanished. Unfortunately, some centuries-old petroglyphs have been damaged by senseless acts of vandalism. Park visitors can help protect these irreplaceable archeological treasures by reporting acts of vandalism to a park ranger as soon as possible, including license plate numbers and other pertinent details.

An ancient petroglyph defaced by graffiti near the South Entrance of Zion.

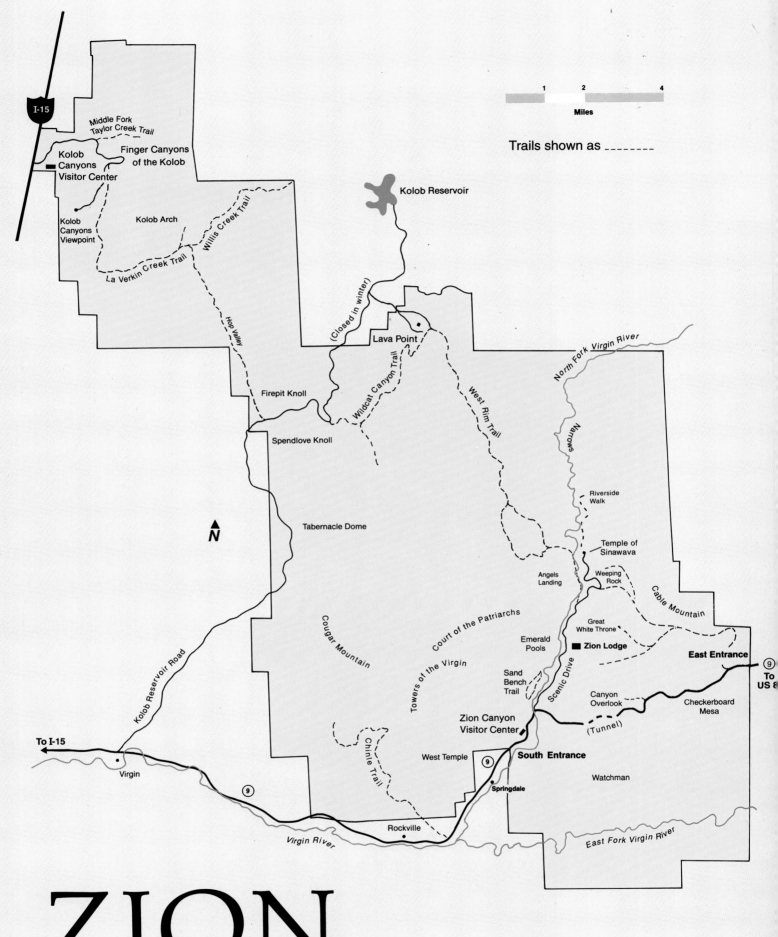

I-15

Middle Fork
Taylor Creek Trail

Kolob
Canyons
Visitor Center

Finger Canyons
of the Kolob

Kolob
Canyons
Viewpoint

Kolob Arch

Kolob Reservoir

La Verkin Creek Trail

Willis Creek Trail

Hop Valley

(Closed in winter)

Lava Point

North Fork Virgin River

Firepit Knoll

Wildcat Canyon Trail

West Rim Trail

Narrows

Spendlove Knoll

Riverside
Walk

Temple of
Sinawava

Tabernacle Dome

Angels
Landing

Weeping
Rock

Cable Mountain

Court of the Patriarchs

Great
White Throne

Cougar Mountain

Emerald
Pools

Zion Lodge

East Entrance

9

To
US 8

Kolob Reservoir Road

Towers of the Virgin

Sand
Bench
Trail

Scenic Drive

Canyon
Overlook

Checkerboard
Mesa

(Tunnel)

Zion Canyon
Visitor Center

To I-15

Chinle Trail

West Temple

9

South Entrance

Watchman

Virgin

9

Springdale

Rockville

Virgin River

East Fork Virgin River

N

Trails shown as _ _ _ _ _ _

1   2   4
Miles

ZION
NATIONAL • PARK